Fr
&
Christmas
2019

Greta Thunberg

Climate Crisis

A Play By

Acie Cargill

Published by Acie Cargill

aciecargill@gmail.com

http://aciecargill.com

ISBN: 9781097609147

Imprint: Independently published

Formatted - Brenda Van Niekerk

brenda@triomarketers.com

Website Design - Brenda Van Niekerk

http://triomarketers.com

Synopsis

Let the children lead us if they know things better than us. The old people should know the most, but there are some things that the kids know better. We all do stuff over and over. Repetitive lives. We go with the easy ways. Because they work for us. The kids don't have all that baggage. They can just see what is right. What is better for the world and life in general. They don't want the old ways. Time to change is now, before it is too late, and the earth will be in uncontrollable decline.

The kids see that. They want to live their whole lives that are ahead of them and they think about the destruction of things they hold dear. Like the forests and the animals and the normal weather patterns. The kids can sense that we are still making things worse. They are in a battle for survival against the established powers who control everything and care more about money than saving this planet for posterity. The kids know that.

About the Author

Acie Cargill is a poet, a songwriter, and a prose writer. He studied poetry with USA Poet Laureate Mark Strand and Illinois Poet Laureate Gwendolyn Brooks. He studied novel writing with Thomas Berger, who wrote Little Big Man (that Arthur Penn made into a movie with Dustin Hoffman in the lead role). Cargill also studied journalism with instructor Jean Daily. His work is a synthesis of all these styles.

He is a member of American Mensa and formerly Edited the Mensa Journal of Poetry. He also is a member of the Grammy Association, and The US Quill and Scroll Society.

Cargill is a vegetarian, a former holistic physician, a musical performer on a variety of instruments, an environmental activist, a lecturer, medical reviewer, a lover, and a seer.

Website

http://aciecargill.com

Contact

aciecargill@gmail.com

Other Books Written by the Author:

Puerto Rico

Aberrations

Chronicles

Terrorism

Modern Love

Ends and odds

Illiana: The Border Area Between Illinois and Indiana

Pullman

Che and Fidel - A Reading Play of the Cuban Revolution

Celia Sanchez - A Play of the Cuban Revolution

Paschke - A Play

Gwendolyn Brooks: A Play

Rasputin - A Play

Nietzsche - A Play

Bob Dylan, The Early Years - A Musical Play

Michael Jackson - A Play

Einstein - A Biographical Play

El Chapo - A Play In 3 Acts

Raisins and Roaches - A Three Month Diary of a Crack Addict

Susan B. Anthony - A Biographical Play

Kankakee

Harriet Tubman - A Biographical Play

Tesla - A Biographical Play

Vegan Saint - A Play in 3 Acts

Martin Luther King, Jr - A Play

Great Migration: A Play in 3 Acts

George Pullman - A Play in Three Acts

Frederick Douglass - A Biographical Play

Freud - A Biographical Play in 3 Acts

The Underground Railroad - An Educational Play

Payton, Jordan, Ali - A Biographical Play

Mr. Nobody - A Play

The Kid From Left Field - A Play

Puerto Rico, A Dream of Independence - A Play in 3 Acts

Crack Madness - A Monologue Play

Johnny Appleseed - A Family Play

Dr. Jekll and Mr. Hyde - A Modernized Play

Obama - Obama - A Play In 3 Acts

Will Rogers - A Biographical Monologue

Merle Haggard - A Biographical Monologue

Mother Teresa - A Biographical Monologue

Gwendolyn Brooks - A Biographical Monologue

Love Life of Susan B. Anthony - A Monologue Play

Sojourner Truth - A Biographical Monologue plus Narrator

Harriet Tubman and The Underground Railroad - A Play

Helen Keller, Words and Wisdom - A Biographical Play

Eugene Debs and the 1894 Pullman Strike - A Play

The Rising - A Play

Walt Disney - A Biographical One Act Play

The Experiments of Dr. Victor Frankenstein - A Play - Based on the novel by Mary Shelley

Karl Marx - A One Act Play

Martin Luther at The Diet of Worms - A One Act Play

Martin Luther King: Monologue and Narrator Play

Frederick Douglass - Monologue and Narrator Play

Kaepernick - A One Act Play

Settling South Holland - A Play In 2 Acts

Kaepernick - A Full-Length Play

My Son Died From An Overdose - A Play

Overdose - A One Act Play

Always a Marine First

Erotic Muslim Polygamy

George Dolton's Bridge to Freedom Underground Railroad - A One-Act Play

Skit List

Scene 1

Greta

We are now facing a crisis. A climate crisis causing an ecological crisis. Our house is on fire. Our house is coming apart. We are about 11 years away from when our climate breakdown will become irreversible. Our civilization is being sacrificed for a small number of people to make enormous amounts of money. The people in power are getting away with not doing anything about the climate crisis. We will make sure they will not get away with it any more.

I had had enough. I sat in front of the Swedish Parliament with a sign for the climate. I called for a school strike. We want the politicians to join us in the street and our protests instead of flying around the world and adding to the problems. There is nothing about the climate in the breaking news and headlines, but It is an emergency.

We are in the midst of the sixth mass extinction. It is 1,000 times faster than ever before with up to 200 species becoming extinct every day. We must take 2 steps back for the sake of all living species. We children have all of our lives ahead of us. We want the adults to act. We want our hopes and dreams back.

We are facing much suffering by an enormous amount of people. Now is not the time for speaking politely. Now is the time to speak clearly. There is no time to continue down this road of madness. Do not concentrate on what is politically easy. Concentrate on what needs to be done or there is no hope. Politicians have ignored us before and will ignore us again. They are running after excuses and we are running after time. Elections are coming up soon, but people like me are not allowed to vote.

They talk about moving forward, but they have the same bad ideas that got us into this mess. The only sensible thing to do is put on our emergency brakes. The politicians must start acting like we are in an emergency. They talk about reducing emissions, but the world is increasing them. They only think of things that add to economic growth because they are afraid of being unpopular. I don't care about being popular. I care bout climate justice and our living planet.

Time is running out. We have started to take action to clean up your mess and we will not stop until we are done. They say we are fighting for our future, but we are fighting for everyone's future. They say we are not mature enough to have much to say about things. If the children all over the world unite, we will have a lot to say. We will never stop fighting for our futures. For the future of our planet and for the future of our children and grandchildren. I want us to act like our house is on fire, because it is.

Scene 2

Svante Thunberg

Yes, I am Greta's father. I was an actor in Sweden and her mother was a fairly well-known operatic singer. We were successful enough to afford a wastefully large house in Stockholm and two luxury cars. We ate a lot of meat and neither of us really cared much about the environment or the ideas behind climate change. That is especially surprising for me because I am descended from and named after Svante Arrhenius, who won the Nobel Prize in 1903 for his study of the greenhouse gases, particularly carbon dioxide, and its global warming effect on our climate. In fact, he is known as the "Father of Climate Change". And to be honest, I just wasn't interested in what climate change really meant until Greta made me become aware of it.

She was 8 years old and withdrew from our reality. She stopped talking. Not just to her parents, but she didn't talk to anyone for over 3 years. There were hundreds of cases of this happening to children in Sweden, usually from refugee families. It is some kind of depression where the child progressively withdraws from their world. Usually there are no deaths because the parents feed and tend to the child. Often, the child sleeps most of the time. It is just some sort of a depression and just giving up on the world. Maybe from lack of encouragement.

Greta remembers her teacher at school talking about climate change and the more she thought about it, the more discouraged she became about the Earth's future and of course, about her personal future. She lost her zest for life and retreated into her own mind. I call the effect optosis. She just didn't want to live anymore. She withdrew more and more.

We didn't know what to do so we let her stay home from school. In the meantime, she spent all her time studying about climate change. She became a vegan to avoid being part of animal suffering. The next thing I knew is she convinced me, and also her mother, to be vegans.

We sold our cars and got an electric car and we moved into a smaller house with much less carbon footprints. Yes, solar powered, of course. My wife and I both gave up our careers because our travel and lifestyles offended Greta's burgeoning interest in being non-destructive to life and the earth. Eventually, after several years, she started speaking again because she realized that she wanted to help fight against climate change. We became a vegan, pro-earth family. Yes, green all the way.

Let the children lead us if they know things better than us. The old people should know the most, but there are some things that the kids know better. We all do stuff over and over. Repetitive lives. We go with the easy ways. Because they work for us. The kids don't have all that baggage. They can just see what is right. What is better for the world and life in general. They don't want the old ways. The time to change is now, before it is too late, and the earth will be in uncontrollable decline. The kids see that. They want to live their whole lives that are ahead of them and they think about the destruction of things they hold dear. Like the forests and the oceans, and the animals, and the normal weather patterns. The kids can sense that we are still making things worse. They are in a battle for survival against the established powers who control everything and care more about money than saving this planet for posterity. The kids know that.

Scene 3

Greta

This is my message to President Trump of the United States. When I was about 8 years old, I heard about something called climate change. Apparently, that is something that humans had created by our way of living. I knew a little about conservation of resources. I had been taught previously to turn out the lights and recycle paper to save energy.
If burning fossil fuels is so bad that it threatens our very existence, then how can we just continue like this. Why were there no restrictions? Why wasn't it made illegal. To me it didn't add up. When I was 11, I became ill. I fell into a depression. I stopped talking and I stopped eating. In two months I lost 20 pounds of weight. I only spoke when I thought it was necessary. Now is one of those moments.

Some of us like me see everything in black and white. We don't enjoy any lying and we don't play social games. I think most people are strange, especially when it comes to the sustainability crisis. They consider climate change to be an importan t thing, but thejust carry on as before.

I don't understand that. If the emissions have to stop, then we must stop the emissions. To me that is black and white. There are no gray areas when it comes to survival. Rich countries must reduce their emissions by 15% per year so we can stay in our target reductions to prevent global warming. I would think our leaders and the media would be talking about nothng else, but they hardly ever mention it. Nor does anyone ever mention the greenhouse gasses locked in the system. Nor do they speak about the pollution in the air that adds to warming of the Earth.

Our leaders never mention climate justice so that the improvements will be made on a global scale. The rich countries must get down to almost half their emissions. That is so the people in poorer countries will have a chance to heighten their standard of living and improve their infrastructures such as roads, schools, hospitals, and clean drinking water and the reduction of diseases. How can we expect contries like India or Nigeria to care about climate change when we who have everything don't ever even think of it?

Why are we not reducing our emissions? Why are they in fact still increasing. The vast majority of people are not evil. They just don't have a clue about the rapid changes they are causing. They think they would see signs if there really was a crisis. Not just flooded cities, but tens of thousands of dead people and nations with piles of torn down buildings. There would be restrictions, but no one talks about it. There are no emergency meetings, no headlines, no breaking news. Politicians keep flying around the world eating meat and dairy.

What we do right now will affect my life and the lives of my children and grandchildren. My generation cannot undo the destruction of the past, in the future.

When school started, I sat down outside the Swedish Parliament calling for a school strike. Not many of the leaders spoke to me. Most just ignored me. Some said I should be in school studying to be a climate scientist to solve all the problems. But the climate problems have been solved. We know what must be done. We just have to wake up and change. And why should I be studying for the future when soon there will be no more. No one is doing anything whatsoever to save that future.

Some people say it doesn't matter what we do or say. If I can get so much publicity just by not going to school, just think what we could do together all over the world if we wanted to. We do need hope, but the things we have done so far don't work or else the emissions would have gone down by now. We need action more than hope. Once we start to act, then hope is everywhere. Today we use millions of barrels of oil every day. There are no politics to change that. We can't just play by the rules. Everything has to change, and it has start to change today.

Scene 4

Svante

How this all came about? It goes back a few years when Greta felt ill. She stopped eating and stopped talking and fell into a depression. And she stayed home from school almost a year and lost some weight. She went to a hospital. My wife Malena and I gave up our jobs and we stayed home to take care of our two daughters.

When Greta came back from the hospital, she was very concerned and upset about climate change and it stuck to her and she couldn't get it out of her head. Especially that everyone seemed to be saying one thing and doing the exact opposite all the time. Not the least was us, her parents. We were two very concerned parents. We were outspoken on human rights and helping refugees. We were very concerned about taking care of our fellow citizens, but we were missing out on one big point. The most important point. The climate sustainability crisis going on around us.

Here we were talking about taking care of our fellow man and we were flying around and eating meat, buying things and driving big cars. We had two homes. Then we realized we were a huge part of the problem. In fact, we were the problem. Greta could not get around that, and it made her very upset. She told us we had to change, and she began showing us many statistics.

My wife had flown to Japan to do concerts that were important to her, but Greta said you just spent 20 people's carbon budget. And we were doing the same thing at conferences for human rights. Greta said you cannot keep doing that working towards human rights while you are living this lifestyle. So, we gave up that lifestyle. No more flying and we became vegans.

Greta was becoming very frustrated because the politicians were saying things about the climate being the most important issue, but the emissions were still rising. So, then she decided to go on a school strike.

Our leaders say one thing and do another or probably do nothing at all. Humans have been doing double lifestyles as long as there have been humans. First say love thy neighbor and then go out on the battlefield and kill each other. We can't do this double lifestyle anymore. Times up. The budget has been spent. It's as simple as that. With the situation we have today, you have to get out there, leave the regular methods, get off the map. Do new stuff.

Scene 5

Interviewer

What is the most surprising thing you have found out about climate change?

Greta

The most surprising thing is that people don't know they are in this situation. We all say that we know, and we think that we know, but we don't know. We know some things. We know that the planet is warming because of the greenhouse gases caused by humans. We don't know the exact consequences of that, and we don't know the rapid changes required to stop it. I've met politicians and journalists that don't have a clue. They don't know any of the basic facts of climate change.

Interviewer

Your knowledge on the climate is like 6 standard deviation beyond the knowledge of an average journalist. So, I can understand that they don't know things you might talk about.

Greta

Politicians like to talk about a carbon budget and how many more years we have. That is all false. We have already spent our carbon budget and we are borrowing from future generations and their lives will be more difficult.

Pollutants of 350 parts per million is the safe threshold and we crossed that line in 1987. So now we are looking for magic solutions that don't exist yet. Basically trees. But we keep cutting more and more trees. It is not a good situation.

Interviewer

Most people will not be able to understand the facts and figures that you know. What do you think is the best way to get people to act?

Greta

It is up to the media to make people think it is important. Treat it as an emergency. Front page headlines. Stories every day because this is so important. The journalists have to be more active themselves. We say there are no black and white issues. But there are black and white issues. Survival is a black and white issue. Climate change is a black and white issue. We need the journalists to take responsibility and get it done. Do whatever it takes. Do it if you can't do it.

Interviewer

What 's next? What will you do next in your quest to save this planet from being destroyed by ourselves.

Greta

I don't know for sure, but I am going to sit outside the Swedish Parliament every friday until Sweden is n line with the Paris agreement on the climate crisis. Whatever happens, happens.

Interviewer

What I think will happen is that tens of thousand or hundreds of thousands of students around the world will join you in your protests. In fact, many students in many countries are staying out of classes on Fridays to protest the climate changes. What can we do to make a difference?

Greta

It won't make a difference if one person stops flying or burning coal or eating meat, but it will make other people think and change their ways also. And that would make a difference if many people change. We must lead by example. Practice what we preach.

Scene 6

Greta

I am honored to be asked to speak today to this European parliament. Tens of thousands of students are school striking on the streets of Brussels. Hundreds of thousands of students are striking around the world. There are school strikes because we have done our homework. People tell us that they are so hopeful. They are hopeful that the young people are going to save the world, but we are not. There is simply not enough time to wait for us to grow up and become the ones in charge.

By the year 2020, we need to have bent the emissions curve steeply downwards. We know that most politicians don't want to talk to us, but we don't mind because we don't want to talk to them either. We want them to talk to the scientists instead. Listen to them. We are just repeating what the scientists have been saying and have been saying for decades.

We want them to follow the Paris Agreement and the IPCC report. We demand that they unite behind the science. When many politicians talk about the school strike for the climate, they talk about most anything except the climate crisis. They claim that our school strike is promoting truancy and we should go back to school. They make up conspiracies and call us puppets who cannot think for ourselves. They are desperate to change the subject and take the focus from the climate crisis. They don't want to talk about it because they know they cannot win this fight. They know they haven't done their homework, but we have.

Once you have done your homework you know we need new politics and new economics where everything is based on our declining carbon budget, but that is not enough. We need a whole new way of thinking. The political system we have created is all about competition. All that matters is to win and get power. That must come to an end. We must stop competing with one another. We must work together and share the resources of the planet.

We need to protect the biosphere, all living species, the air, the soil. The oceans and the forests. We must devote our entire beings on climate change because if we fail to do so then all our challenges and achievements have been for nothing. All that will be left of our politicians' legacy will be the greatest failure in human history and they will be remembered as the greatest villains of all time. They have chosen not to listen and not to act.

This does not have to be. There is still time. We are about 11 years away from being in a position where we set off an irreversible chain reaction beyond human control. To avoid that we have to make changes throughout our society within this coming decade, including a reduction of our emissions by at least 50% by the year 2030. Any less will not be enough of a reduction to protect our future generations.

Some people say we are fighting for our future, but that is not true. We are fighting for everyone's future. Saying everything will be all right while doing nothing is not hopeful to us. In fact, it is the opposite of hope.

And don't say we are wasting valuable lesson time. The politicians have wasted decades of lesson time and they still have not learned. Join us in the streets and our protests. We have started to clean up your mess and we will not stop until we are done.

Made in the USA
Monee, IL
11 December 2019